REMEMBER 10 WITH EXPLORER BEN

CATHERINE VEITCH   ILLUSTRATED BY **DUNCAN BEEDIE**

WITH MEMORY TECHNIQUES BY

TRACY PACKIAM ALLOWAY, PHD

Copyright © QEB Publishing, 2017
Part of The Quarto Group
6 Orchard, Lake Forest, CA 92630

First published in the United States in 2017 by QEB Publishing

A CIP record for this book is available
from the Library of Congress.

ISBN 978-1-68297-206-9

Publisher: Maxime Boucknooghe
Editorial Director: Laura Knowles
Art Director: Susi Martin
Designer: Verity Clark

Originated in Hong Kong by Bright Arts

Printed and bound in China by
Toppan Leefung Printing Ltd

10 9 8 7 6 5 4 3 2 1

17 18 19 20 21

CONTENTS

CEREAL BAR

A Memory-boosting Adventure

> This book combines a fun adventure story with a memory game, and along the way, it teaches children a variety of techniques to help them boost their memory.

Follow Explorer Ben on a journey around the world, stopping off at exciting places such as the desert and the Arctic. Each journey is split into two parts.

In the first part, Ben shows the reader the ten things he needs to pack, and the reader is introduced to a Memory Tip to help them remember those ten items.

In the second part, butter-fingered Ben has lost some of his things! He needs the reader's help to remember what's gone missing! As the book progresses, the challenges get harder, as Ben loses more of his belongings.

WHY DO I WANT TO HELP MY CHILD IMPROVE THEIR MEMORY SKILLS?

It has been shown that training your memory helps to improve focus and concentration. Creative memory techniques also enhance problem-solving abilities and creative thinking. Equipped with these skills, children become better learners. Improved memory techniques have also been shown to enhance children's social skills, as they increase children's confidence and their ability to remember instructions and make independent decisions.

EXPLORING THE BOOK WITH YOUR CHILD

While older children might like to explore the book independently, younger children may need support to master each memory technique and help Explorer Ben remember which items he's lost, so make it into a fun game. At the end of the book, parents will find notes on further ways they can help their child improve their memory and concentration.

Hello explorers! Grab your backpacks and come on an adventure with me, Explorer Ben!

I'm off on a journey around the world, but there are so many things I must remember to pack.

Ben needs to take 10 things to the Amazon Rainforest. Can you help Ben remember everything he needs to pack? Use the MEMORY TIP to help.

flashlight

binoculars

sleeping bag

insect spray

compass

pocket knife

Up, up, and away! First stop: the Amazon rainforest.

water bottle

tent

book

EXPLORE THE AMAZON

hat

MEMORY TIP
Make up a funny picture for each thing, as funny pictures are easier to remember. Here are some silly pictures for Ben's water bottle and his compass.

book

hat

EXPLORE THE AMAZON
EXPLORE THE AMAZON

flashlight

tent

pocket knife

insect spray

8

Off to the Arctic now! Thanks for remembering my binoculars. They will be useful on this adventure too.

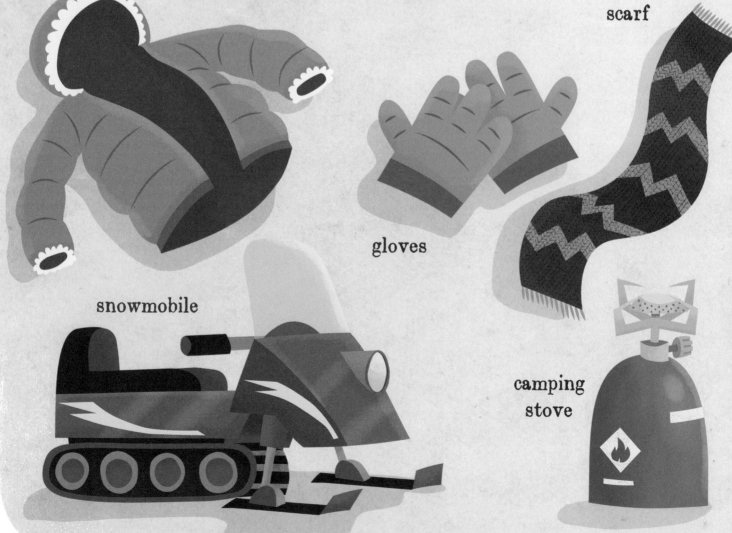

Remember 10 things to take on Ben's Arctic adventure.

coat

scarf

gloves

snowmobile

camping stove

Leap onto my snowmobile and come along for the ride. Whoa! Hold on tight!

boots

camera

book

THE ARCTIC

vegetable soup

goggles

MEMORY TIP
Make up a little story that includes all ten things. Remember this story or make up one of your own.

Ben read a BOOK about the Arctic. Then he ordered a SNOWMOBILE, some GLOVES, GOGGLES, and a SCARF. Next he cooked some VEGETABLE SOUP on his CAMPING STOVE for lunch. Then the doorbell rang. Ben looked out of the window and saw that his order had arrived. He put on his COAT and BOOTS and rushed outside with his CAMERA to take a photo of his new, shiny snowmobile.

gloves

coat

camera

book

THE ARCTIC
THE ARCTIC

boots

?

I need to go somewhere warmer now. This camel will be great for exploring my next place, but I hope he behaves!

book

THE DESERT

THE DESERT

camel

sunglasses

spade

Remember 10 things to take on Ben's desert adventure.

sun hat

CEREAL BAR

cereal bar

sunscreen

50

bucket

fan

headscarf

MEMORY TIP
Make up a little rhyme that includes all ten things. Remember this rhyme or make up one of your own.

Give me my BOOK,
And let's take a look
At the hump-backed CAMEL
—what a funny animal!
Grab my SUNGLASSES and my SUN HAT,
My SUNSCREEN too—but just a pat.
Here's my BUCKET and my SPADE.
See the sandcastles I've made.
If I get hot, there's my HEADSCARF and FAN,
I'll bring a CEREAL BAR too,
that's a very good plan!

camel

?

headscarf

That naughty camel dumped me in the waterhole and I lost THREE things in the water. Can you remember what's missing?

cereal bar

?

spade

?

bucket

book

sun hat

THE DESERT

I'm super excited to go on Safari next, where I hope to film some amazing animals. Jump in my jeep and come along.

SAFARI

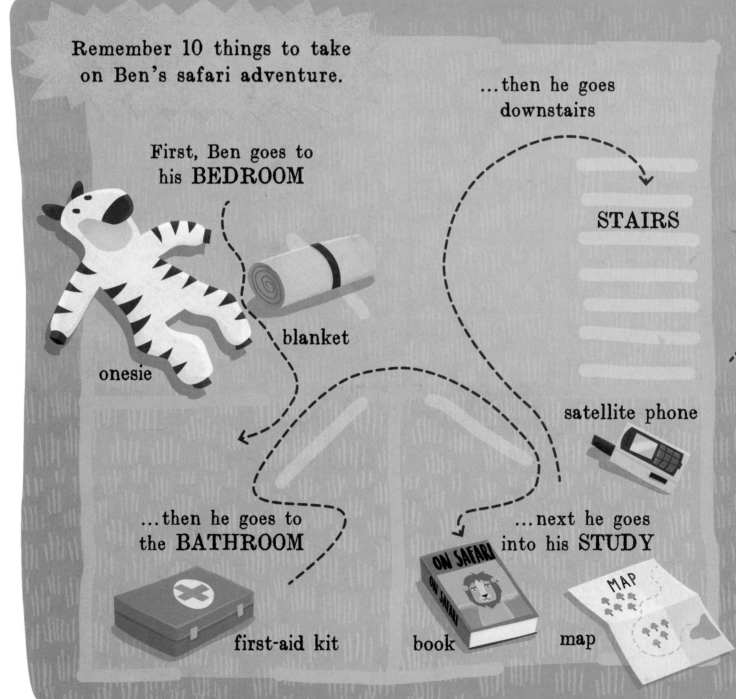

Remember 10 things to take on Ben's safari adventure.

First, Ben goes to his **BEDROOM**

...then he goes downstairs

STAIRS

onesie

blanket

satellite phone

...then he goes to the **BATHROOM**

...next he goes into his **STUDY**

ON SAFARI

MAP

first-aid kit

book

map

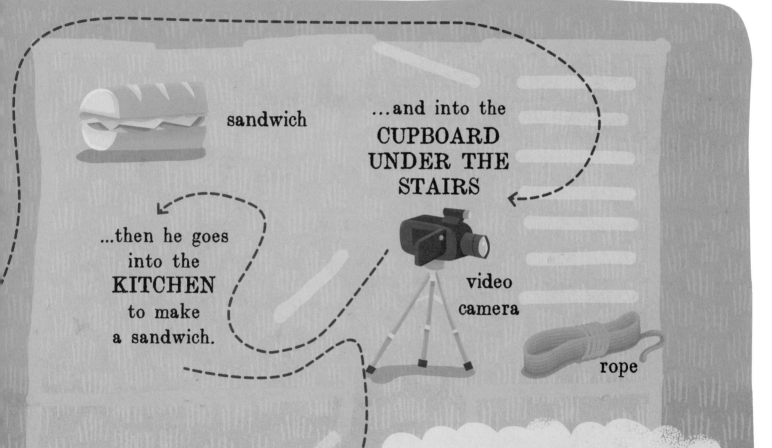

sandwich

...and into the
**CUPBOARD
UNDER THE
STAIRS**

...then he goes
into the
KITCHEN
to make
a sandwich.

video
camera

rope

...Finally, Ben goes
into the **GARAGE**.

jeep

MEMORY TIP
Close your eyes and
imagine Ben walking around
his house to pick up all ten
things. Imagine this journey
or a journey around
your own home.

jeep

?

rope

video
camera

?

onesie

?

Oh dear, I lost FOUR things while I was filming. Can you remember what's missing?

blanket

?

first-aid kit

I'm off to climb a mountain next. Jump aboard this train and we'll be there in a flash!

Remember 10 things to take on Ben's mountain adventure.

book

MIGHTY MOUNTAINS

MIGHTY MOUNTAINS

jacket

walking pole

pom-pom hat

列車チケット

ticket

kettle

skis

boots

ski poles

whistle

MEMORY TIP
It's easier to remember things when they are in pairs. Remember these pairs, or make up some of your own.

SKIS	—	you also need SKI POLES
BOOTS	—	better with a WALKING POLE
TICKET	—	in the pocket of the JACKET
BOOK	—	fits inside the POM-POM HAT
WHISTLE	—	KETTLE: both make a noise!

boots

jacket

walking pole

Ahoy me hearties! Are you ready to go snorkeling with me? All right then, let's set sail.

Remember 10 things to take on Ben's snorkeling adventure.

flag

cheese

swim ring

MEMORY TIP
Make up a picture in your mind of each thing on Ben.

Imagine Ben in his WETSUIT, wearing his FLIPPERS, SNORKEL, FACE MASK, LIFE JACKET, and a SWIM RING. He carries a FLAG, and has a CAMERA around his neck, while reading his BOOK and eating CHEESE!

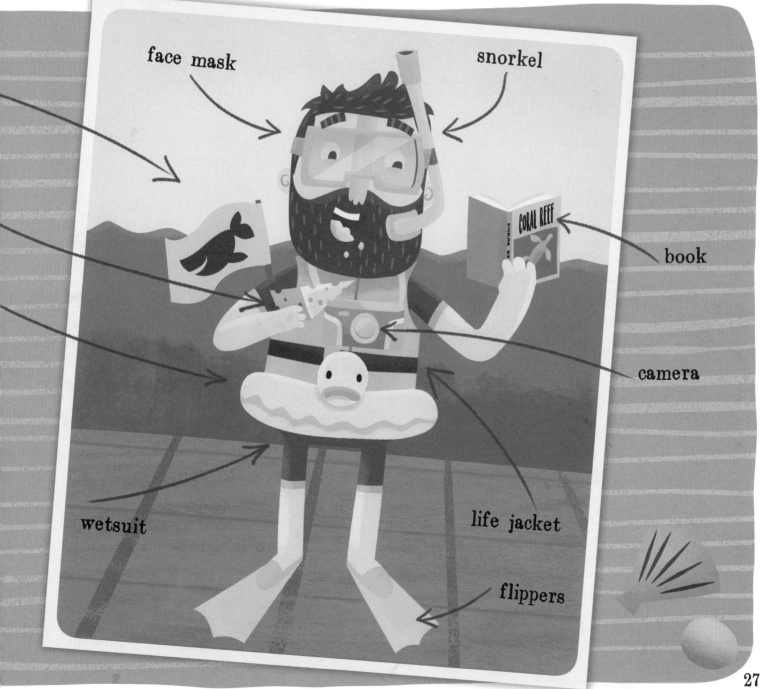

face mask

snorkel

book

camera

life jacket

wetsuit

flippers

snorkel

Some mischievous pelicans stole SIX of my things. Can you remember what's missing?

?

flippers

wetsuit

flag

It's good to be on dry land! Next I'm going by helicopter to the outback in Australia.

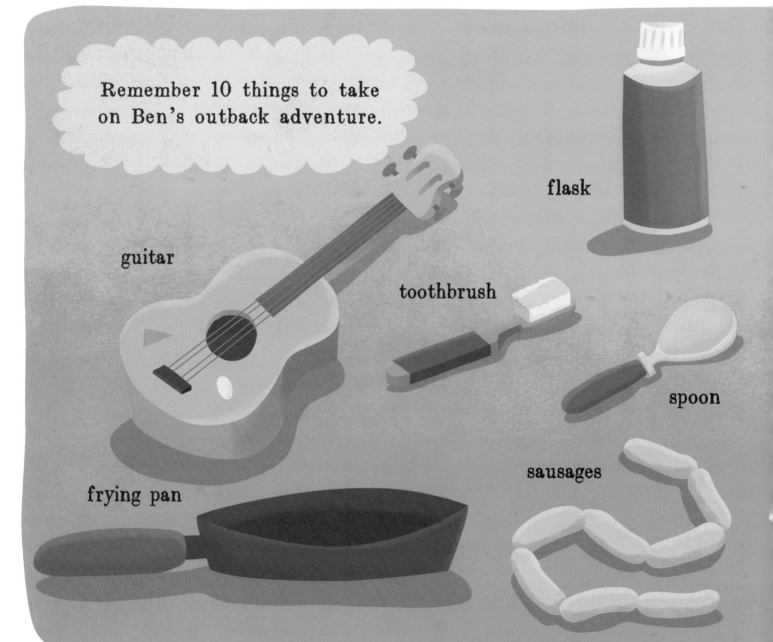

Remember 10 things to take on Ben's outback adventure.

flask

guitar

toothbrush

spoon

sausages

frying pan

plate

mug

toothpaste

book

MEMORY TIP
Act out using each of Ben's ten things. For example, copy these actions, or make up some of your own.

- Play an imaginary GUITAR.

- Open an imaginary FLASK, pour out the drink into a MUG, and lift it to your mouth.

- Fry some imaginary SAUSAGES in an imaginary FRYING PAN.

- Pick up the sausages with an imaginary SPOON and put them on a PLATE.

- Put some imaginary TOOTHPASTE on a TOOTHBRUSH and pretend to brush your teeth.

- Read an imaginary BOOK.

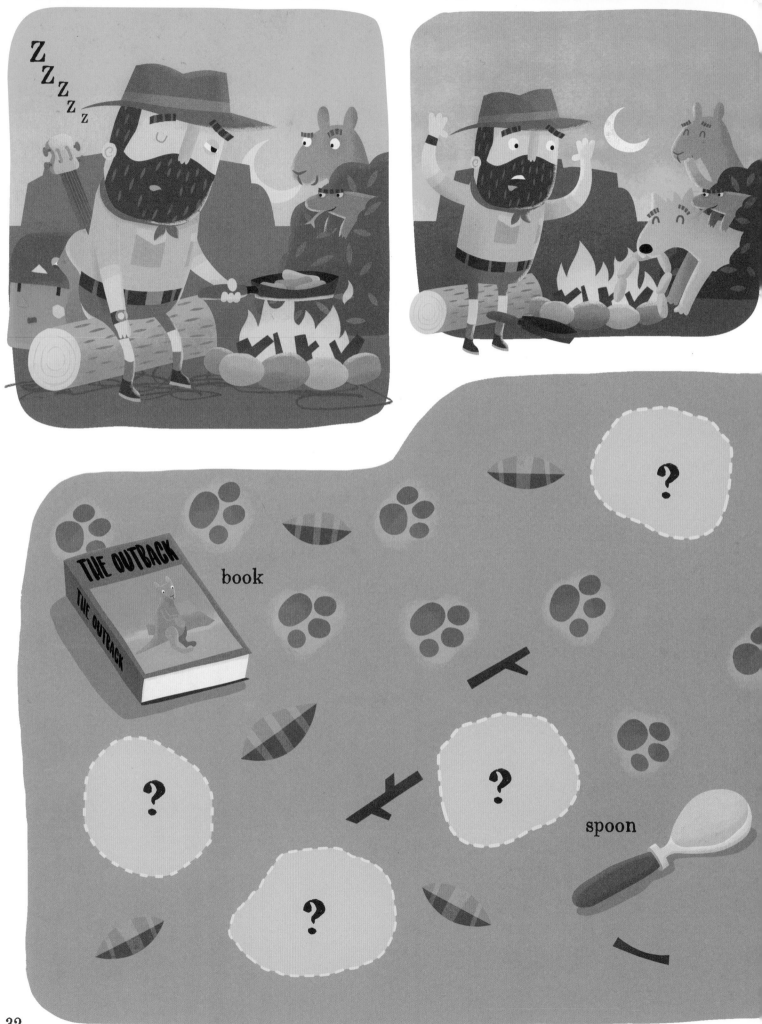

book

spoon

frying pan

Those pesky animals stole SEVEN of my things. Can you remember what's missing?

It's good to get away from that hot weather. It will be cooler exploring this cave.

Remember 10 things to take on Ben's cave adventure.

watch

orange

book

CAVING

CAVING

ladder

helmet

socks

spade

gloves

MEMORY TIP
Match each of Ben's ten things to a color of the rainbow. For example, remember these or make up some of your own.

cable

boots

red CABLE

orange SOCKS and orange ORANGE

yellow BOOTS and yellow GLOVES

green LADDER and green SPADE

blue HELMET

indigo BOOK

violet WATCH

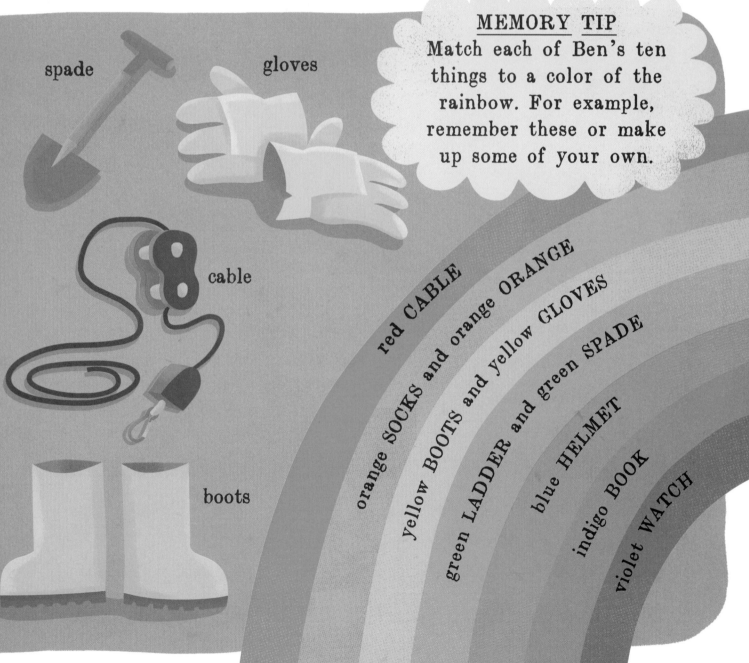

gloves

?

socks

It was so dark and
cramped in that cave
that I lost EIGHT things.
Can you remember
what's missing?

Thanks for helping me find my things. Join me for some white water rafting next, if you dare!

Remember 10 things to take on Ben's rafting adventure.

book

oar

raft

helmet

teddy bear

towel

life jacket

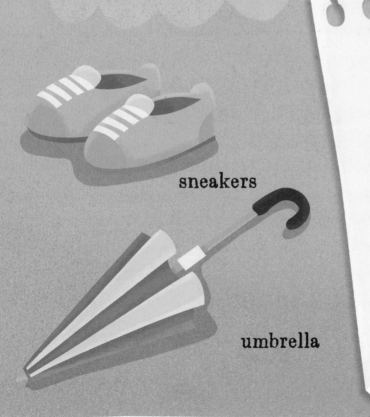

MEMORY TIP
Describe each of Ben's ten
things with a word that begins
with the same first letter.
For example, remember these
descriptions or make up
some of your own.

rubber duck

sneakers

umbrella

big BOOK ✓
rubber RAFT ✓
lovely LIFE JACKET ✓
ugly UMBRELLA ✓
tall TEDDY BEAR ✓
old OAR ✓
hard HELMET ✓
tiny TOWEL ✓
soft SNEAKERS ✓
round RUBBER DUCK

raft

DANGER

41

I can't wait to fly as high as the clouds in my hot air balloon. Come up, up, up, and away with me!

Remember 10 things to take on Ben's balloon adventure.

book

HOT AIR BALLOONS

streamer

chair

teaspoon

table

teapot

cup

tea

milk

MEMORY TIP
Make up a song that
includes all of Ben's ten things.
Remember this song to the tune of
"Twinkle, Twinkle, Little Star," or
make up one of your own.

Flying high up in the air
with my TABLE and my CHAIR.

Bright STREAMER and a pretty view,
a TEAPOT, CUP, and SAUCER too.

Stir the MILK with my TEASPOON,
drinking TEA all afternoon.

I'll read my BOOK and look around,
there's lots to see above the ground.

saucer

Oh dear, I lost all TEN of my things! I'll check the weather before I go hot air ballooning next time. Can you remember what's missing?

THE MOON

Marvelous Memory Quiz

Do you have a
marvelous memory?
Take this quiz
to find out.

1. Ben made up funny pictures to remember his things in the Amazon Rainforest. What was the picture he made up for his water bottle?

A)   B)   C)

2. What snowy creature made Ben jump in the Arctic?

A)   B)   C)

3. Ben made up a rhyme with the things he took to the desert. Which word would you choose to help you remember your coat?

A) Rabbit   B) Goat   C) Bear

4. Which two animals did Ben spot on safari?

A)   B)   C)

5. It helped Ben to remember his things in pairs. Can you remember what he paired with his ski poles for the mountain?

   A) Bucket   B) Kettle   C) Skis

6. Which two sea creatures did Ben meet on his snorkeling trip?

   A)   B)   C)

7. Ben acted out using the things he took to Australia. Do some actions that will help you to remember these things.

   A) Jelly   B) Bathtub   C) Clock

8. Ben matched each thing he took caving to a color. Can you remember which color Ben matched his socks with?

   A) Yellow   B) Blue   C) Orange

9. Ben matched each thing he took rafting to a word with the same first letter. Which word would you choose to help you remember your toothbrush?

   A) Long   B) Tickly   C) Smelly

10. Ben's hot air balloon was in the shape of an animal. Can you remember what it was?

   A) Cat

   B) Bear

   C) Fish

Don't worry if you couldn't answer all the questions. The more you practice, the better your memory will be!

ANSWERS: 1=B; 2=A; 3=B; 4=B and C; 5=C; 6=A and B; 8=C; 9=B; 10=B.

47

TIPS FOR PARENTS

Here are five more steps you can take to help improve your child's memory skills (and your own!). All of these are scientifically proven to benefit memory and concentration.

1. SLEEP ON IT

Learning just before bedtime is a great way to boost memory of that information. Studies show that a good night's sleep after learning helps the brain consolidate and remember new information better compared to when you learn it in the morning.

2. GO BLUE

A healthy diet is crucial for optimal brain function, but some foods have been shown to be especially good for your memory. Blueberries don't just taste great—they're also a bit of a wonder fruit when it comes to boosting memory. Multiple studies have found that the flavonoids in this fruit are the reason behind cognitive benefits at all ages.

3. CLIMB A TREE

Scientific research has shown the cognitive benefits of being "proprioceptively dynamic." That sounds fancy, but it means doing physical activities such as crawling, balancing, and climbing trees. Just two hours of this sort of physical activity can improve working memory by 50 percent... and it's good for your body too!

4. DOODLE

Doodling while you work on a boring task can actually improve attention and working memory, according to one study. When you doodle, you are less likely to daydream or lose interest in the task.

5. DARK CHOCOLATE

This last tip might surprise you. Give your child dark chocolate to satisfy their sweet tooth. Studies show that people who ate dark chocolate (70% cocoa solids or higher) were more accurate in working memory tests and also responded faster compared to those who ate white chocolate. Just don't eat too much!